Mountains of Jokes About Rocks, Minerals, and Soil

Laugh and Learn About Science

Written by Melissa Stewart

Illustrated by Gerald Kelley

Enslow Elementary, an imprint of Enslow Publishers, Inc.

Enslow Elementary® is a registered trademark of Enslow Publishers, Inc.

Library of Congress Cataloging-in-Publication Data
Stewart, Melissa.
  Mountains of jokes about rocks, minerals, and soil: laugh and learn about science / written by Melissa
Stewart; illustrated by Gerald Kelley.
      p. cm. — (Super silly science jokes)
  Includes index.
  Summary: "Learn about minerals, the Earth's layers and plates, lava and more. Read jokes about all
of these topics, and learn how to write your own"—Provided by publisher.
  ISBN 978-0-7660-3969-8
  1. Minerals—Juvenile literature. 2. Rocks—Juvenile literature. 3. Minerals—Juvenile humor.
4. Rocks—Juvenile humor. I. Kelley, Gerald, ill. II. Title.
  QE365.2.S743 2011
  549.02'07—dc23

                        2011026528

Future editions:
Paperback ISBN 978-1-4644-0165-7
ePUB ISBN 978-1-4645-1072-4
PDF ISBN 978-1-4645-1072-1

Printed in China

012012 Leo Paper Group, Heshan City, Guangdong, China

10 9 8 7 6 5 4 3 2 1

To Our Readers: We have done our best to make sure all Internet Addresses in this book were active
and appropriate when we went to press. However, the author and the publisher have no control over
and assume no liability for the material available on those Internet sites or on other Web sites they may
link to. Any comments or suggestions can be sent by e-mail to comments@enslow.com or to the address
on the back cover.

Illustration Credits: © 2011 Gerald Kelley (www.geraldkelley.com)

Photo Credits: © 2011 Photos.com, a division of Getty Images, pp. 7 (left), 27, 31, 36; Enslow
Publishers, Inc., p. 44; Photo Researchers, Inc.: David Hardy, p. 11, Gary Hincks, pp. 12;
© iStockphoto.com/Claudia Dewald, p. 25 (top); Shutterstock.com, pp. 1, 4, 7 (right), 8, 14, 16, 19,
20, 23, 28, 32, 35, 38, 39, 40, 43.

Cover Illustration: © 2011 Gerald Kelley (www.geraldkelley.com)

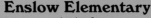

Enslow Elementary
an imprint of
Enslow Publishers, Inc.
40 Industrial Road
Box 398
Berkeley Heights, NJ 07922
USA
        http://www.enslow.com

Contents

Let's Rock!

You see **rocks** around you every day. They're under your feet and along the side of the road. They're in buildings and jewelry and even chalk.

Rocks are closely connected to minerals and soil. Rocks are made of minerals. And **soil** contains bits of broken up rock.

As you read this book, you'll learn all kinds of cool facts about rocks, minerals, and soil. But that's not all. This book is also chock full of jokes. Some of them will make you laugh out loud. Others might make you groan. (Sorry.) But either way, you'll have a good time. So let's rock!

Q: What did the angry rock say to the sassy soil?

A: "Come on! You want a piece of me?"

Q: What do rocks eat for dessert?

A: Marble cake.

Q: What did the rabbit say to the rock?

A: "You're too hard to get along with."

2 Minerals Matter

What's a **mineral**? That's a good question. Gold is a mineral. So is a diamond. But what exactly does that mean?

A mineral is a natural solid material. But it's not alive. And it never has been.

Believe it or not, a mineral has something in common with chocolate chip cookies. These cookie favorites always contain the same mix of ingredients. Minerals do, too.

The atoms that make up a mineral have something in common with the twelve eggs in a carton. The eggs are always arranged in the same pattern. So are the atoms. That means every sample of a mineral, such as gold, looks exactly the same—both inside and out.

Gold is always made of gold atoms. Diamond is always made of carbon atoms. But most minerals contain two or more atoms. Quartz contains two atoms—silicon and oxygen.

Q: Who is a mineral's favorite fairy tale character?

A: Goldilocks.

Q: What kind of babies do diamonds have?

A: Carbon copies.

3 Layers of Earth

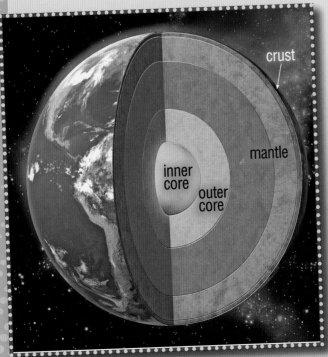

crust

mantle

inner core

outer core

Most of our planet is made of rock. But the planet is not a hard, solid ball.

Earth is made of layers, just like a birthday cake. The top layer is called the **crust**. Like the frosting on a cake, Earth's crust is thin compared to the layers below it.

Next comes a thick layer called the **mantle**. It contains hot, soft rock called **magma**. Even though magma is thick, it can flow—just like cooked oatmeal.

Earth's sizzling-hot core has two parts. Melted metals slosh around inside the liquid outer core. The weight of all the overlying layers presses the inner core's molecules close together. So the inner core is solid.

Q: What does Earth have in common with a piece of bread?

A: They both have a crust.

Q: What does Earth have in common with an apple?

A: They both have a core.

Magma on the Move

Would you believe that Earth has something in common with a mug of hot cocoa? It's true.

When you hold a steaming mug of cocoa, heat flows from the chocolate drink to your hands. The same thing happens inside Earth. Heat flows from the core to the mantle.

All that heat warms up the magma at the bottom of the mantle. And that causes the magma to move up toward Earth's surface. At the same time, cooler magma sinks down to take its place. Over millions of years, magma slowly circles through the mantle.

What does moving magma have to do with rocks? Keep on reading to find out.

Q: Why does magma move in circles?

A: It doesn't want to be square.

Q: What did the mantle say to the inner core?

A: "You're hot stuff!"

inner core

outer core

mantle

mantle

crust

Warm magma rises up from the bottom of the mantle. Cooler magma sinks to take its place.

11

The Puzzle of Plates

Okay, let's start off with a joke: What does Earth's crust have in common with a dinner table? Give up? They both have plates.

Don't get it? That's probably because Earth's **tectonic plates** don't look anything like dinner plates. Earth's plates are giant slabs of rock. They fit together like the pieces of a puzzle.

Guess what happens to the plates as magma circles through Earth's mantle? They go along for the ride. That's right! The plates move across the surface of the planet. They float on top of the mantle like rafts on a sea of moving magma.

On average, Earth's plates move about two inches (five centimeters) a year. Your fingernails grow at about the same rate.

The Earth's surface is divided into nine major plates. The pink arrows show the direction the plates move.

Q: Why did the North American Plate get in trouble?

A: He made a false move.

WANTED

North American Plate

Guilty of False Moves

Last seen in the company of the Pacific & Eurasian Plates

Q: How does the mantle find out what's happening on Earth's surface?

A: It reads magmazines.

 Vibrant Volcanoes

Think all magma stays locked inside the mantle? Think again.

In some parts of the world, plates are pulling apart. Magma rises to the surface and spills out through cracks.

In other places, plates are crashing together. Sometimes one plate slides below the other. Then the lower plate melts and forms new magma. Some of that magma forces its way to Earth's surface and erupts through cracks.

What do scientists call those cracks? Volcanoes.

Magma that gushes onto Earth's surface is called **lava**. Erupting lava is hot stuff—up to 2,200°F (1,200°C). But the instant lava hits air or water, it starts to cool. It doesn't take long to harden into **igneous rock**. *Igneous* comes from a Latin word that means "fire."

Q: What did one volcano say to the other volcano?

A: "I lava you."

Q: How do igneous rocks celebrate Independence Day?

A: They watch fireworks.

7 Cool as a Crystal

Ever hear of basalt? It's an igneous rock that forms from lava. It cools so quickly that it doesn't have time to form **crystals**.

Granite is an igneous rock, too. But it looks totally different. It has lots of little crystals inside. They may be gray, white, pink, and black.

Why does granite have crystals? Because the magma it's made of didn't blast out onto Earth's surface. It might have been stuck at the top of the mantle. Or maybe it was trapped inside the crust. The magma cooled slowly. And it formed igneous rock full of crystals.

Some igneous rocks contain big, beautiful crystals. Diamonds can form inside kimberlite. Sapphires and rubies can be found inside pegamite. These valuable crystals grow slowly over thousands—or even millions—of years.

Granite

What a Gem!

Looks like it's time to start off with another question: What's the difference between a crystal and a **gem**? Answer: All gems are crystals. But not all crystals are gems.

Confused? Don't be. A gem, or gemstone, is a large, hard, beautiful crystal. It's been cut and polished, so it can be used to make jewelry.

Fluorite and calcite are beautiful crystals. But they're too soft to be made into gems. They scratch easily, so people don't use them in jewelry. You probably know the names of some popular gems. There's diamond, sapphire, ruby, and emerald. Amethyst, topaz, and turquoise are popular too.

Q: Why did the emerald raise his hand?

A: Because the answer was crystal clear.

Q: What did Ruby's grandmother tell her?

A: "Sweetheart, you're a real gem!"

9 Wear and Tear

Everyone knows rocks are hard. But guess what? Wind and water can be even tougher.

Crashing ocean waves can slowly **erode**, or wear away, rock. So can fast-flowing rivers and whipping winds.

Rocks can break when plant roots grow into cracks. Acid rain and snow can make rocks weak. Over time, the rocks slowly crumble into tiny bits. In places with cold nights and hot days, rocks freeze and thaw, freeze and thaw. This **weathering** can make rocks shatter.

See? Rocks aren't all they're cracked up to be.

Q: Why did the little pebble look so much like the big boulder?

A: It was a chip off the old block.

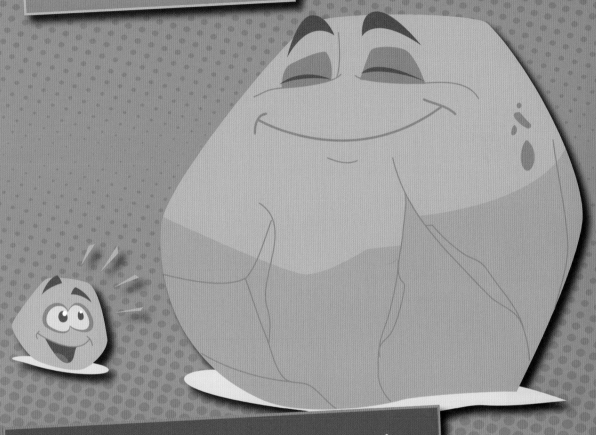

Q: What did the rock say when the wind refused to go to bed?

A: "You're wearing me down."

10 The Secrets of Soil

You see soil every day. But have you ever wondered exactly what it's made of? Here's your chance to find out.

The recipe for one measuring cup—8 ounces (240 milliliters)—of average soil is:

- 3.5 ounces (105 ml) of broken-up rock

- 2 ounces (60 ml) of water

- 2 ounces (60 ml) of air

- 0.5 ounces (15 ml) of **humus**—rotting bits of plants and animals

There may not be much humus in soil. But it has an important job to do. It's food for lots of little creepy crawlies. Earthworms, beetles, and centipedes live in soil. So do fungi and **bacteria**. Even plants get nutrients from humus.

Q: Why was the humus upset?

A: Because everyone was treating him like dirt.

Q: Why was the farmer dirt poor?

A: He didn't have a single cent-ipede in his soil.

One! Two! Three!

Think all soil is the same? Well, it's not. According to scientists, there are three different kinds.

Soil with large bits of rock is called sand. Silt has medium-sized bits. And clay has the smallest bits of all. In fact, you'd need a microscope to see them. Now that's small!

Go outside and grab a handful of soil. Squeeze it, and watch what happens.

Add a little water to your soil, and squeeze again. What happens now?

Here's how you'll know what kind of soil you have:

Mostly Sand	Dry	Feels gritty, falls apart
	Wet	Holds together but crumbles easily
Mostly Silt	Dry	Feels smooth and silky, holds together
	Wet	Holds together but cannot be rolled
Mostly Clay	Dry	Holds together but cannot be rolled
	Wet	Holds together and can be rolled

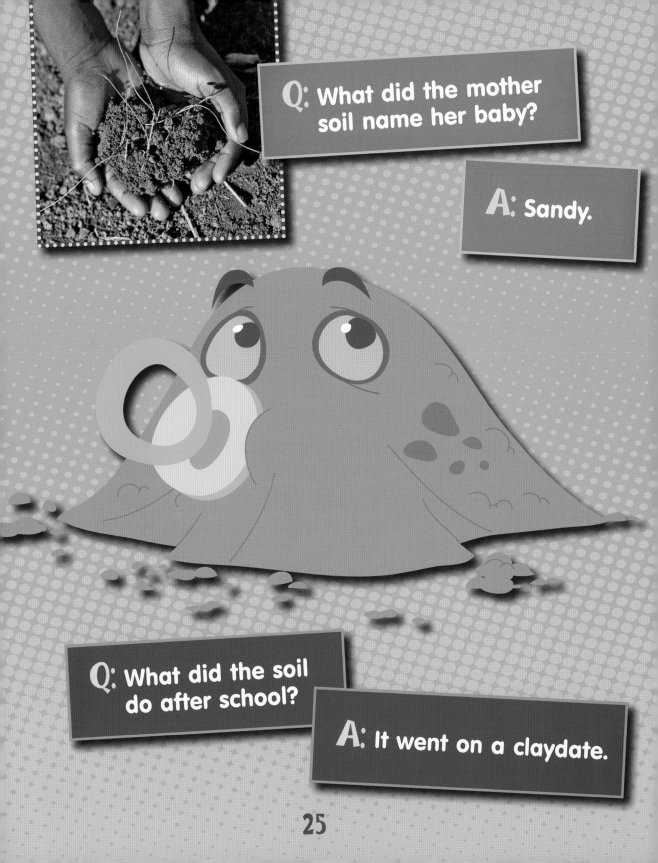

Q: What did the mother soil name her baby?

A: Sandy.

Q: What did the soil do after school?

A: It went on a claydate.

25

12 Layer by Layer

When you gulp a glass of water, it's hard to imagine the liquid's incredible power. It can slowly demolish rocks. And it can carry the broken bits to brand-new places. Rivers and streams can also wash away sand, silt, and clay. All these sediments travel downstream to oceans and lakes.

As time passes, the sediments build up—layer by layer by layer. The weight of the materials on top presses down on the lower layers. All that pressure squeezes out the water. Then it cements the sediments together to form **sedimentary rock**.

Sedimentary rock is the most common kind of rock on Earth's surface. If you look closely at sandstone, limestone, or shale, you might be able to see its layers.

Q: What do rocks say when they agree with one another?

A: "My sediments exacty."

Q: What did the sedimentary rock say to the hairdresser?

A: "Give me lots of layers."

13 Sedimentary Stories

Believe it or not, sedimentary rocks can tell tales. Really, they can.

Ripples in sandstone show which way the wind was blowing or water was flowing when the sediments were deposited. The colorful walls of the Grand Canyon hold clues about how the temperature and climate of the area have changed over time.

And that's only the beginning. Many sedimentary rocks contain fossils—evidence of past life. Dinosaur bones, shark teeth, and leaf imprints are **body fossils**. They show us what life was like millions of years ago.

Grand Canyon

Ancient footprints, **coprolites** (fossilized animal dung? ew! gross!), and unhatched eggs are **trace fossils**. They tells us how ancient creatures lived. Studying body fossils and trace fossils together gives scientists the clearest view of the ancient world.

Q: What happens when a dinosaur dies angry?

A: It becomes a hostile fossil.

Grrr...

Q: What is the opposite of a coprolite?

A: Young dung.

14 A Peek Inside Caves

Ready for another riddle? What can be as small as a telephone booth or as big as a mountain? This time the answer is easy: A cave.

Not every natural opening in the ground is a cave. It must be big enough to hold a person.

Many caves form in limestone. First, water seeps into cracks between its layers. Then chemicals in the water slowly eat away at the sedimentary rock. As time passes, the cracks grow wider and deeper. Eventually, large tunnels and rooms form. Years later, the water drains out and the cave fills with air.

Sometimes icicle-shaped **stalactites** grow down from the ceiling of a cave. Stubby **stalagmites** may grow up from the floor. They make caves beautiful places to visit.

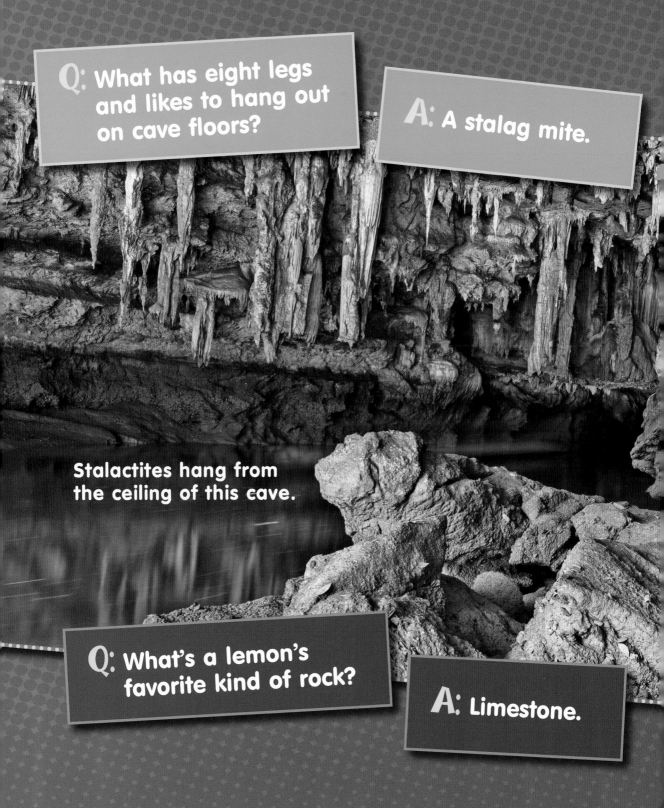

Q: What has eight legs and likes to hang out on cave floors?

A: A stalag mite.

Stalactites hang from the ceiling of this cave.

Q: What's a lemon's favorite kind of rock?

A: Limestone.

15 Burst and Bake

Hope you've been paying attention. It's time for a quick quiz. What happens when magma gets stuck in Earth's crust?

That's right. It cools slowly and forms igneous rock full of crystals.

But what about the surrounding rock? How does the burst of fiery magma affect the rocky crust all around it? As the magma cools, it gives off heat. Lots and lots of heat. Enough heat to bake nearby rock and change the minerals inside. The result is a new kind of rock—a **metamorphic rock**. *Metamorphic* comes from a Greek word that means "to change form."

Q: Why did the sedimentary rock invite the magma to come visit?

A: It was ready for a change.

EASY BAKE METAMORPHIC

JUST ADD HEAT!

Q: Why did the magma accept the invitation?

A: The trip would give it a chance to chill out.

Making Mountains

Metamorphic rock can also form in another way. Remember those tectonic plates moving across Earth's surface? Well, sometimes they pull apart. And sometimes they crash together.

Two things can happen when plates crash together. Sometimes one plate slides down below the other one. Other times, the two plates keep on pushing and shoving. They ram and slam into one another year after year. Finally, the edges of the two plates begin to rise. They lift the land to form a mighty mountain.

The rocks inside the growing mountain are twisted, folded, and squeezed. All that pressure changes the minerals inside. And metamorphic rock forms.

Q: Why did the young mountain pull his sister's hair?

A: He wanted to get a rise out of her.

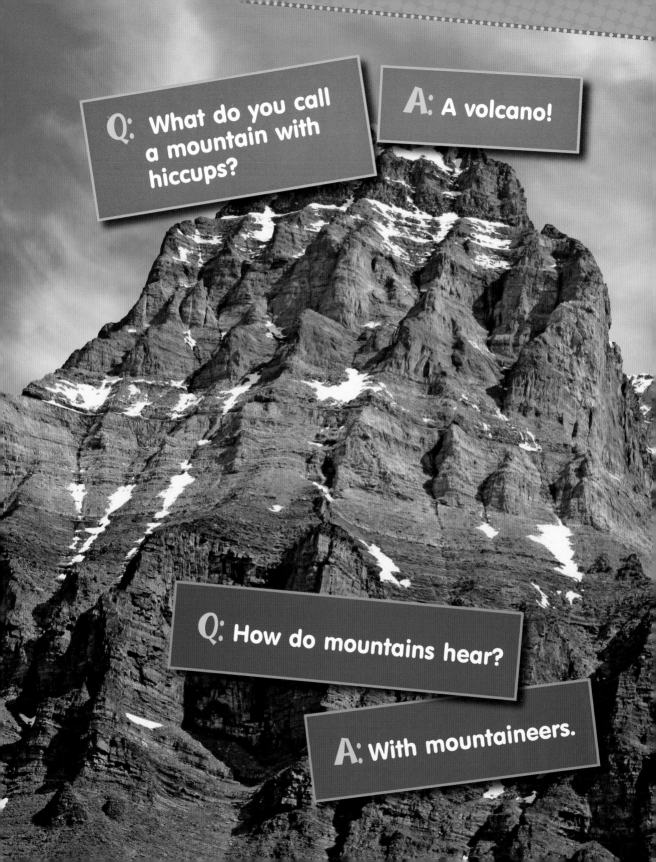

17 Recycling Rock

Think the rocks you see today have always existed? Think again. New rock is forming all the time. And old rock is always breaking down.

As Earth's plates crash together, some rock is twisted and squeezed to form metamorphic rock. Other rock melts to form magma. When that magma blasts out of a volcano, new igneous rock forms.

As time passes, wind and water wear rock down into bits of rock and soil. Rivers and streams wash the pieces into lakes or the ocean. Slowly, the layers build up and form new sedimentary rock. Rocks keep on changing in a never-ending cycle. That's one of the reasons they're so interesting to study.

This rock in Utah is called Delicate Arch. Wind and water made a large hole in it.

Q: Where did the volcano go on Saturday night?

A: To a rock concert.

Q: Why do sedimentary, igneous, and metamorphic rocks get plenty of exercise?

A: They're always on a tri-cycle.

How to Write Your Own Jokes

Writing jokes isn't hard if you keep three helpful hints in mind:

1. Try to think of a joke's punch line, or answer, first. Then work backward to come up with the setup, or question.

2. Keep the setup short and simple. People who listen to your joke will want to try to guess the answer. That's half the fun. But if the question is too long, your listeners won't be able to remember it all. They'll feel frustrated instead of excited.

3. Keep the answer short and simple too. That way it will pack more of a punch.

Popular Expressions

Ever hear someone say: "I'm pooped!" or "He was pooped"? It means the person is tired. He or she needs a rest.

Can you can use this popular expression as the punch line for a joke? You bet!

A coprolite is fossilized animal dung. And what's another word for dung? That's right, "poop." Here's how you can use that information to write a great joke:

Q: Why did the coprolite take a nap?

A: Because it was pooped!

Can you think of another joke that uses a popular expression as a punch line?

Homographs and Homophones

A homograph is a word with two or more different meanings. One example is the word *bright*. It can mean "smart" or "shining."

You can create a question that seems to use one definition of the word and an answer that uses the other. Here's an example:

Q: **Why do diamonds always do well on tests?**

A: **Because they're so bright!**

Homophones are two or more words that sound the same, but are spelled differently and have different meanings. For example, the words *nice* and *gneiss* (the kind of metamorphic rock that forms when granite is exposed to heat or pressure) are homophones.

You can create a great joke by mixing homophones. Here's an example:

Q: What happens to granite when the heat is on?

A: He turns into Mr. Gneiss (NICE) Guy.

These jokes are fun because your family and friends might be able to guess the answers. And sometimes they'll come up with different answers that are just as good. Then you'll have some brand-new jokes to tell someone else.

You can have lots of fun using homographs and homophones to create jokes that will amuse your friends.

Similar Sounds, Different Meanings

Changing a few little letters can also result in words that sound almost the same, like *lion* and *lying* or *cheetah* and *cheater*. And these word pairs can be the inspiration for some hilarious jokes.

Here's an example:

Q: Should silicon and oxygen be friends?

A: Of quartz!

This joke works because the word *course* sounds similar to the word *quartz*.

Can you think of some other jokes that use similar-sounding words? Give it a try.

Rhyme Time

Playing with words to create rhymes can be highly entertaining. It's even better when a rhyme is the heart of a joke. Here's an example:

Q: Where does a metamorphic rock go to take a bath?

A: A mountain fountain.

Getting Silly

Sometimes the best jokes are ones that are just plain silly or ridiculous. Get ready to laugh out loud—here are some great examples:

Q: When does most weathering occur?

A: At the crack of dawn.

Q: Why did the magma stop circling through the mantle?

A: It was getting dizzy.

Your Jokes in Print

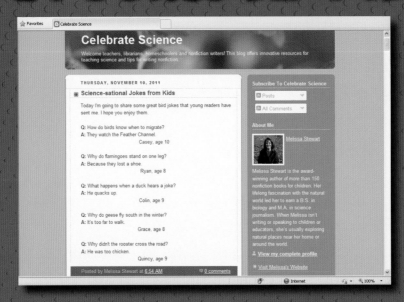

Now it's your turn. See if you can come up with some seriously silly jokes of your own. Then share them with your family and friends.

You can submit your most science-sational jokes to:
mas@melissa-stewart.com
Be sure to include your first name and your age.

The best jokes will be posted on Fridays at:
http://celebratescience.blogspot.com
People all over the world will be able to read and enjoy them. You can send drawings too. Now get to work on some jokes, and don't forget to have a good time!

Words to Know

bacterium (pl. bacteria)—A tiny, one-celled living thing that reproduces by dividing in half.

body fossil—The hardened remains of a plant, animal, or other creature that was once alive.

coprolite—Fossilized animal dung.

crust—The outer layer of Earth.

crystal—A natural solid material made of atoms and molecules arranged in a repeating pattern.

erode—To slowly wear away rock or other materials by the action of wind, water, or ice.

gem—A beautiful crystal that has been cut and polished.

humus—The rotting material in soil.

igneous rock—A kind of rock that forms when magma cools and hardens.

lava—Magma that spills out onto Earth's surface.

magma—Hot, soft rock found below Earth's surface.

mantle—The layer of Earth between the crust and outer core. It is made of soft rock called magma.

metamorphic rock—A kind of rock that forms when heat or pressure changes the minerals in igneous rock or sedimentary rock.

mineral—A natural solid material with a specific chemical makeup and structure.

rock—A natural solid material made of minerals.

sedimentary rock—A kind of rock that forms as layers of soil and bits of rock build up and are pressed and cemented together.

soil—A mixture of broken-up rock, air, water, and rotting plant and animal material.

stalactite—A buildup of minerals that hangs down from the ceiling of a cave.

stalagmite—A buildup of minerals that grows from the floor of a cave.

tectonic plate—One of the large slabs of rock that makes up Earth's crust.

trace fossil—Evidence of how an ancient creature lived.

weathering—The breaking down of rock by plant roots or repeated freezing and thawing.

Learn More

Books

Bollard, John. *Scholastic Children's Thesaurus.* New York: Scholastic Reference, 2006.

Tomecek, Steve. *National Geogrpahic Kids Everything Rocks and Minerals.* Washington, DC: National Geographic, 2011.

Young, Sue. *Scholastic Rhyming Dictionary.* New York: Scholastic, 2006.

Internet Addresses

Mineralogical Museum at Harvard University
<http://www.fas.harvard.edu/~geomus/collections.htm>

Rock Hounds: Discover How Rocks Are Formed
<http://www.fi.edu/fellows/fellow1/oct98/create/>

This Dynamic Planet
<http://www.minerals.si.edu/tdpmap/>

Index